A Light-Hearted Look at the Desert

A Light-Hearted Look at the Desert

Chuck Waggin

The University of Arizona Press

About the Artist

Chuck Waggin, artist for a Tucson television
station for a number of years, has also done
the art work for an Arizona-Sonora Desert
Museum nature series appearing in a Tucson
newspaper. He enjoys working in all media
in the field of art — usually on the humorous
side. He has always been a nature lover and
has found the desert a never-ending source of
ideas and inspiration for his artistic creations.

Eighth printing 1984

THE UNIVERSITY OF ARIZONA PRESS

Copyright © 1969
The Arizona Board of Regents
All Rights Reserved
Manufactured in the U.S.A.

I.S.B.N.-0-8165-0208-0
L.C. No. 74-101697

My wife, Carol,
has helped me greatly
with this undertaking —
in observations,
in research,
in rhymes.

I wish to thank her
for her interest,
for without it
this book would never
have become a reality.

Contents

The windows of our house are like color television sets. We switch from one subject to another simply by switching from one window to another — and with no commercial interruptions. From one window we observe a cactus wren building a nest; from another, we see quail bringing their young ones to share in the seeds we scatter; and from yet another, we watch hummingbirds sipping nectar from feeders and from plants that attract them.

Oftentimes a comedy is played before our eyes, as when we saw a neighbor's cat being chased through the desert by a roadrunner, or a large Gila woodpecker comically swinging upside down on the tiny hummingbirds' feeder and sticking his unbelievably long tongue into the honey nectar.

Many times during the day Mr. Roadrunner taps gently at our kitchen window with his beak, or, with his unmistakable voice, he calls for a handout — pieces of meat that we save for him. He has become tame enough to take food from our hands.

Ground squirrels thrive in our yard and become plump on bits of leftovers. In the spring we see the mother ground squirrels bringing their babies out of the burrows into the sunshine, and we watch their playful antics. The ubiquitous cottontails and jackrabbits help with our lawn mowing. Occasionally a Gila monster will amble through our yard. Although coral snakes are said to be rare, even they have called on us several times.

In the evenings, coyotes come to drink — also owls and other nocturnal creatures. After summer rains, spadefoot toads serenade us. Our fountain is a favorite dunking spot for a few rather stout Colorado River toads.

We find it hard to believe some of the fearsome stories we hear about the desert dwellers. Not one of these creatures — except perhaps a gnat or a mosquito — has ever gone out of its way to attack us. We do not disturb them, and they do not disturb us. Because of our close association with some of these animals, our desert living has become pleasurable and interesting and informative.

We would like to share some of our pleasures with you — through the medium of this book. How does a layman select information for a book? Well, in the case of this layman, it was done by many trips to museums, much reading, wandering around in the desert, sketching, observing, taking pictures, and being fortunate enough to live in an area where many of the subjects make their homes.

Not all the animals and plants grouped together in the drawings in this book will, under natural circumstances, be found in association with one another. The groupings were arranged to produce entertaining situations, or to illustrate certain common characteristics of some of the desert dwellers.

The backgrounds in the illustrations are caricatures of our desert landscapes. Because the western deserts abound with descriptive and picturesque names, such as Eagle Peak, Castle Rock, Shiprock, and Rainbow Bridge, some of the rock formations and mountains in the drawings take on these shapes.

It would, of course, be impossible in a book of this kind to include all animals, plants, birds, reptiles, and insects that inhabit the Southwest. Not only are there many kinds of desert dwellers, but most species include numerous varieties that live in the part of the desert to which they are especially adapted. The subjects chosen for this book are believed to be among those most commonly known, or the most interesting.

This book has several aims: to offer a little dry humor, to give enjoyment, to be interestingly informative, to increase awareness of and interest in the desert dwellers, and, most of all, to kindle a desire to protect the desert and its inhabitants for the enjoyment of our own and future generations of mankind.

CHUCK WAGGIN

A Light-Hearted Look at the Desert

The Desert

Deserts of the Southwest support many kinds of life — many kinds of bushes, shrubs, grass, trees, and flowers, and a large variety of birds, reptiles, mammals, insects, and even fish.

Rivers and lakes are found in the Southwest, and the land elevations range from small sand dunes to pine-forested mountains.

All deserts are not sun and sand,
With old bones cluttering the land.
Deserts are dry; yes, that is true,
But many things can live there, too.

Rock Formations

Nature has sculptured many spectacular rock formations in the Southwest, using as her tools the wind, rain, sand, heat, and cold.

These rocks often seem to take on identifiable shapes — many sorts of amusing and grotesque figures, and many beautiful forms like cathedrals, ships, bridges, and windows.

Golden Eagle

The desert's largest bird of prey, the golden eagle, has a wingspread to seven feet. Its plumage is dark brown, with golden neck feathers. This eagle eats rabbits and ground squirrels and carrion. It builds huge nests at heights inaccessible to most other creatures.

Young eagles at one time were kept in captivity by the Hopi Indians. The white feathers, found only on young birds, were used in Hopi religious rites.

The golden eagle and all other eagles are now protected by a 1963 act of Congress.

Extremes of weather
and wind blowing sand
Make the strange shapes
that you see in this land.

[14]

Roadrunner

A famous resident of the Southwest, and as cuckoo as they come, the roadrunner is a large black, gray, and white streaked bird with a black-crested head. He is a member of the cuckoo family, and is sometimes called a chaparral cock. His voice is a dovelike coo, or sometimes a clack of the beak. The roadrunner prefers running to flying, although he does soar short distances. His nest is built in a bush, tree, or cactus. His food consists of lizards, snakes, insects, and occasionally small birds and rodents.

Sidewinder

The sidewinder is so called because of its sideways motion, which gives good traction in the sand. It is also called a horned rattlesnake, because of hornlike projections over its eyes. From about eighteen to twenty-four inches in length, the sidewinder is a light-colored snake that blends well with the sandy desert where it lives. Rarely seen in the daylight hours, it hunts rodents at night.

Collared Lizard

The colorful lizard with black collars around its neck has background colors ranging from brown to bright green, tinged with yellow or orange. The animal is four to four and one-half inches long, with a tail of eight to nine inches. It can run on its hind legs, and it will bite if molested. Small lizards and insects make up its diet.

Creosote Bush (upper left)

The creosote bush derives its name from the fact that the bush gives off an odor much like creosote, especially after a rain. The roots are believed to exude a substance from their tips that kills nearby plants competing with it for water. The small evergreen leaves of this bush are coated with a resin that helps conserve moisture. The bush blooms in April and May, with small yellow flowers that later form into fuzzy white seedballs.

Is that a tiny dinosaur
Racing o'er the desert floor?
No, it's a lizard making tracks,
In case the roadrunner attacks.

Gila Monster

Largest lizard in Arizona, the Gila monster is protected by law to prevent its extinction. This animal is one of the only two poisonous lizards in the world. The other one is the beaded lizard of Mexico.

The Gila monster has a pink-orange and black, beaded appearance, and he may grow to two feet in length. He seems sluggish but can bite quickly and hang on tightly, although he will not do so without provocation.

On the prowl, chiefly at dusk and later, this lizard hunts for eggs, reptiles, and small rodents. During hibernation he lives on food stored in his tail.

Gecko

A harmless fellow, the gecko, is often mistaken for a baby Gila monster. He appears almost transparent and has a smooth skin and large eyes. When molested, he emits a high-pitched squeak. His name comes from the sound he makes. He is nocturnal and is an insect eater.

Hedgehog Cactus

The hedgehog cactus grows in clumps, and reaches up to eighteen inches in height. It is the first cactus to bloom in the spring, with flowers ranging from pinkish lavender to purple. The juicy red fruit is eaten by birds and rodents.

The gecko said, "I fail to see
Why people think you look like me.
I wish they'd take a better look,
So I won't so often be mistook."

Jumping Cactus

The jumping cactus, also called the tree cholla, has cylindrical joints. With just a slight touch, the loose branching segments seem to "jump" and become stuck on anyone or anything. Many visitors to the Southwest have become attached to this cactus. When segments fall to the ground, they take root. Dense, forestlike stands of these cacti are often found, with fruits hanging in long chainlike clusters.

Engelmann Prickly Pear

A common cactus, the Engelmann prickly pear has flat or padlike joints. The plant grows fast and lives about twenty years. Its blooms are large yellow flowers. Its purplish pear-shaped fruits, called "tunas," are edible when fresh and are sometimes used in making jelly. Desert animals and birds also eat the fruit.

Kangaroo Rat

An odd-looking little creature, the kangaroo rat has very small front legs and feet, but extra long, powerful hind legs and feet which enable him to leap like a kangaroo. With the use of his long, tufted tail, he can change directions while leaping — a great help in eluding and confusing an enemy.

He is nocturnal and eats seeds and plant material. He is one of the few animals in the world that can live without drinking any water. Because of a chemical process in the digestion of food, he obtains moisture from the seeds he eats.

The kangaroo rat is himself on the menu of many predators.

Jumping cactus?
It's a fable!
Can't attack us;
Isn't able!

Harris Ground Squirrel

A common desert dweller, the little Harris ground squirrel resembles a chipmunk. He has gray fur with lighter gray underparts and a white stripe on each side of the body. (A similar species is the antelope ground squirrel.) When danger is near he flicks his bushy tail, which he carries curved over the body.

His call sounds like a bird trill.

He is a vegetarian and is fond of the fruit of the barrel cactus.

Rattlesnake

The rattlesnake is one of the five dangerous denizens of the desert; the others are the black widow spider, the Gila monster, the scorpion, and the coral snake.

The Western Diamondback, the largest rattlesnake in the Sonoran Desert country, will try to avoid humans. If cornered he will strike, and he does not have to coil to do so. Also, he does not always rattle a warning. A good rule for humans to follow, in desert country, is never to put your hands or feet where your eyes can't see.

The rattlesnake can't stand excessive heat. He stays in the shade during the heat of the day and is most active at night, searching for rodents, lizards, and rabbits.

The furry folk
Don't like the joke.
Squirrel's full of sport;
His time is short!

Pyrrhuloxia (top left)

A slender relative of the cardinal, the pyrrhuloxia is fairly common in the Southwest. It has a red crest on its head, and a rosy patch around the beak. Its gray body has areas of red on breast, wings, tail, and thighs. The yellow beak is parrot-like. The female of the species is not as colorful as the male.

The pyrrhuloxia builds its nest in thorny bushes and trees. It eats seeds and some cactus fruits.

Cardinal (right)

Except for a black patch around his conical beak, the crested male cardinal is completely red. The female is yellow-brown, with a pointed crest and thick reddish bill. The cardinal eats seeds and insects.

Phainopepla (bottom left)

The name phainopepla means shiny cloak. Indeed, the bird is a shiny, slim, black fellow with a tall crest and white wing patches that are noticeable in flight. The eyes are red.

This bird builds its nest in or near desert mistletoe. Its food consists of berries and insects.

Three pretty desert birds are we,
Perching here in this old dead tree.
Each of us has a feathered crest.
Which one of us do you like best?

Centipede

The centipede attains a length of six to eight inches. It has one pair of legs per body segment, and a sharp claw on the tip of each leg.

This creature can inflict a painful bite, but it is not dangerous. It is useful as a destroyer of insects.

Millipede

A wormlike arthropod, the millipede has two pairs of legs to most body segments. He curls up when disturbed so that the hard plates of the back protect the leg area.

The millipede discourages his enemies by exuding a substance from stink glands. He is harmless however.

After summer rains the millipede can be seen crawling on the surface of the ground. Its food is decaying plant matter.

The centipede and millipede
Do have many legs indeed.
Found mostly after summer rains;
Remind one of small speeding trains.

Raccoon

The appealing little raccoon has a black mask and black-banded furry tail. He makes his home in a canyon, near water if possible. His den is in a tree, in a small cave, or under a ledge.

For food he prefers aquatic animals, but he will eat insects, mice, cactus fruits, and vegetable matter. With his long fingers, he washes his food in water whenever it is available.

Coati

A relative of the raccoon, the coati (or coatimundi) is a rusty brown animal with a long black-banded slim tail that he usually carries erect.

The coati eats tubers and insects and lizards, which he grubs out with his long snout. He will also eat berries and small rodents.

The male is solitary. Females and their offspring travel in small groups. These animals originally migrated into the United States from Mexico.

In Mexico the animal is called *chulo,* which means *cute.*

Chuckwalla

After the Gila monster, the chuckwalla is the desert's largest lizard — about sixteen inches in length, including the tail. He is brownish in color. A harmless animal, he can wedge himself into crevices by inflating his body, making it difficult for enemies to dislodge him.

The chuckwalla is chiefly vegetarian, feeding on cactus fruits and flowers and on desert plants.

At one time the chuckwalla served as food to the Indians.

*"I've no treasure, so can't hand it
Over to this strange masked bandit!"
Coati, don't be such a loon,
This is just a cute raccoon!*

Yucca (at left)

A member of the lily family, the yucca reaches a height of ten to fifteen feet. It produces large clusters of white flowers. It depends on the moth (pronuba) to transfer its pollen. The moth needs the yucca for food for its young, which hatch in the yucca fruit.

Agave

The agave is often called the century plant, because it was once thought to take that long to bloom. Actually, ten to twenty years are required to store enough food to produce the huge flower stalk. After the agave has flowered, the plant withers and dies.

Sotol

Similar to the yucca, the sotol also bears white flowers on a tall spike. This plant, sometimes called a spoon plant, is often seen in flower arrangements. Use of the leaves for this purpose has made the plant scarce in some localities. The taking of desert plants without a license is unlawful.

Nolina

Sometimes called beargrass, the nolina has long grasslike leaves which are used by the Indians in making baskets. The flower stalk is tall but not rigid, and it, too, bears small white flowers.

In silhouette and leaves and spike,
These plants may seem to look alike.
We may think they're all the same,
Until we know each one by name.

Mountain Lion

The mountain lion, a yellowish brown cat with dull white underparts and a long, heavy tail, is also called a puma, panther, and cougar. The male may weigh up to 200 pounds.

This animal once ranged from Canada, through most of North America, to the southernmost part of South America. He keeps mostly to the mountainous regions.

The mountain lion stalks his prey and can leap a distance of twenty feet or more. His favorite food is the deer. He is a beneficial animal, whose feeding habits help keep nature's balance in check.

This cat is afraid of man, his worst enemy.

Pack Rat

The pack rat is also called a trade rat or a wood rat. He collects a variety of items and especially likes shiny things. He may drop whatever he happens to be carrying to trade it for something he likes better. That is why he is sometimes called a trade rat.

His nest is within a large moundlike structure, protected by huge piles of cactus joints. The juicy pulp of certain cacti serves as food and moisture for him. He also feeds on fruits, berries, grass, and seeds.

The pack rat is harmless, and one of the desert's cleanest animals. Many animals prey on the pack rat.

Pack rat, just what is that thing
That you bring to me — your king?
Be off with you! Shoo and scat!
Don't forget, I am a CAT!

Colorado River Toad

The largest toad in the Sonoran Desert, the Colorado River toad, grows to seven inches long and wide. It eats insects, spiders, scorpions, and small lizards.

These toads have skin glands that secrete poison which can be injurious to dogs that try to annoy them.

Eggs are laid in pools of water.

Praying Mantis

Green or brown in color, the praying mantis can effectively hide itself in foliage to prey on unsuspecting insects. The mantis is capable of turning its head from side to side.

The praying mantis derives its name from the attitude of prayer in which it folds its front legs. Food is held with the forelegs.

This creature is at times cannibalistic, but it is perfectly harmless to humans. The female frequently eats the smaller male after mating.

Sacred Datura

The sacred datura, or western jimsonweed, grows along roads and washes. It has large trumpet-shaped white flowers, with dark green leaves and a prickly fruit pod. The plant is poisonous and dangerous if eaten by cattle or by humans.

"Oh won't you stay to dinner?"
Said the mantis to the toad.
"It's such a lovely evening
For a picnic by the road."

White-winged Dove (left)

The white-winged dove is ten to twelve inches in length, has grayish brown feathers, white bars on the wings, and a rounded tail. As this dove goes from blossom to blossom among the saguaros, sampling the nectar, it aids in pollination of the plants. All doves are seed eaters, and most of them eat fruits. The white-wing especially likes the saguaro cactus fruit. In the autumn, the white-wing migrates to Mexico.

Inca Dove (center)

The Inca dove is a small gray bird six to eight inches long, with scaled plumage, rust-colored patches on the wings, and a long slim tail bordered with white on the sides. Doves and pigeons are the only birds that feed their young a milky liquid, called pigeons' milk, formed in the parent's crop. This dove seems to enjoy being near human habitations.

Mourning Dove (right)

A little smaller than the white-winged dove, the mourning dove is brownish gray with a long tapered tail. This common native dove makes a mournful cooing sound — hence its name. When it flies, its wings make a whistling sound. Doves must have water every day, and they sometimes fly considerable distances to find it.

Mesquite Tree

Common in the desert, the mesquite tree grows to twenty-five feet high. It belongs to the pea family, and in the spring has fragrant yellow blossoms. The fruits, resembling green bean pods, when ripened are a favorite food of desert animals.

We think the desert is just dandy,
If we can find some water handy.
And when we find a pond that suits,
Then all we need are seeds and fruits.

Spotted Skunk

The spotted skunk is the smallest and prettiest and most playful of the four species of skunk found in Arizona. The other three are the hooded, striped, and hog-nosed skunks.

The spotted skunk has a black coat, with broken stripes of white, and a bushy black tail with a white tip.

This skunk lives in brush, or in a hollow log, or beneath an old building. He is nocturnal and feeds on rodents, insects, snakes, cockroaches, scorpions, and cactus fruits.

His handstand trick doesn't always mean that he is angry — sometimes it is just play and bluff.

"Hey, guys, watch my feat!"
But his pals all retreat.
Because of, we assume,
His dis-stink-tive perfume.

Tarantula

Tarantulas are the largest of American spiders. They are dark brown, with a hairy appearance. They make their homes in web-lined holes in the ground.

The bite of the tarantula is painful but not serious. They do not bite unless annoyed. These creatures are beneficial to man, as they eat many insects which they find during their nighttime prowling. Tarantulas cannot jump great distances, but they make short leaps when catching insects.

Grasshopper (short-horned)

The grasshopper can leap to thirty inches. He makes his song by rubbing his hind legs against his wings.

Grasshoppers are plant eaters. They themselves serve as food for many desert creatures.

Grasshoppers move with a leap and a bound,
As they go springing all over the ground.
Some people think that tarantulas too
Leap a great distance; but that isn't true.

Bobcat

The bobcat, also known as a wildcat, is the most common species of cat in the Southwest. He gets his name because of his short bobbed tail. He has tufted ears and yellow-brown fur mottled with black spots.

This cat is secretive and not often seen during the day. He does most of his hunting at night, looking for rodents of all kinds, and rabbits. He will climb trees in search of birds.

Ringtail Cat

The ringtail is not a cat; he is related to the raccoon. He is sometimes called a miners' cat because miners used to keep ringtails for pets. His color is brownish yellow-gray, and he has large eyes and ears and a bushy tail ringed in black.

The animal makes his home in a cave or under a ledge near water. A rodent hunter, the ringtail is nocturnal; but he is sometimes seen taking the sun in a secluded spot.

Organ Pipe Cactus

A columnar cactus with ribbed branches growing up to twenty feet or more from ground level, the organ pipe is more common in Northwest Mexico than in Arizona. However, there are stands of these cacti in Southwest Arizona. Also, in Arizona, a national monument has been established to protect this and other desert plants and animals.

The organ pipe is night blooming and has edible fruits.

Rainbow Cactus (lower right)

Not a common cactus, the rainbow is usually found among rocks in the mountains of Southern Arizona. It is called rainbow because of its alternating bands of red and white spines that mark its growth from year to year. It grows to twelve inches in height and has large pink blossoms.

The bobcat sees the ringtail cat
And thinks he'd like a tail like that.
His own is such a little thing.
He'd like one he could flick and fling.

Mexican Freetail Bat

Freetail bats are identified by the tail that projects beyond the wing membranes. These bats are pugnosed and have cup-like ears.

Daytimes the bats spend in caves and under overhanging cliffs. They emerge at night to gorge on insects, consuming vast numbers. These mammals are a great help in keeping down the insect population.

Bats are the only mammals capable of true flight.

White-footed Mouse

The white-footed mouse grows to eight inches in length, including the tail. He resembles a large house mouse, but has large ears, white feet, and a haired tail.

Seeds, plants, fruits, and some insects are food for the white-footed mouse. Because he is nocturnal, he serves as food for almost every night-hunting predator.

The freetail bats are homely things.
They look like mice equipped with wings.
The little mouse, though he's earthbound,
Sure wishes he could leave the ground.

Desert Mule Deer

Mule deer have large ears like a mule, are light gray-brown with white rump patches, and have white tails with black tips. The males have large branched antlers.

These deer live in the open country and desert foothills. When alarmed, they run with a bounding gait.

Mule deer are vegetarians; they eat cactus fruits, grass, leaves, and twigs.

Ironwood Tree

The leaves of the ironwood tree are dark green. The tree blooms in May or June, with beautiful lavender blossoms. Its seeds are eaten by the desert animals.

Because the wood is so solid and hard, it is difficult to work. The tree is becoming scarce in some areas because it is a favored firewood.

Wildflowers

Under favorable weather conditions, the desert in the spring is a carpet of wildflowers — lupin, poppies, mallows, purple-mat, pricklepoppy, desert marigold, desert zinnias — to name a few.

We can see that it is spring —
A butterfly is on the wing,
The ironwood tree sends new leaves out,
The baby mule deer leaps about.

Gambel Quail

Gambel quail are common in the desert. The male has a black patch on a light tan belly, a reddish brown head, and a black face outlined in white. The sides are brown flecked with white, and the rest of the body is gray. Both male and female are plumed.

These quail often raise large families in nests on the ground. The quail chicks can run as soon as they are hatched — resembling tiny "dust bunnies" with legs. These birds eat seeds, desert fruit, and insects.

Desert Tortoise

The desert tortoise is about ten inches long. He is a harmless animal. His speed is about twenty feet per minute.

The tortoise digs a burrow to escape weather that is too hot or too cold; he also uses it for his winter sleep.

He obtains moisture from vegetation, and he has the ability to convert food to water. But he drinks water when it is available.

The desert tortoise may live as long as fifty years.

The Gambel Quail said, "Please do wait
For my children and my mate."
Said Desert Tortoise, "That's okay.
I'm in no hurry anyway."

Arizona Bull Snake

The Arizona bull snake usually grows to four or five feet in length; it may reach seven feet. It has a gray-brown or yellow-tan background color, with red-brown saddle-shaped blotches.

This snake, a constrictor, is harmless but will hiss and strike if cornered.

Because rodents are the bull snake's favorite food, the snake is of value to farmers.

Roundtail Ground Squirrel

The roundtail is most often found where the creosote bushes grow. He is a reddish-tan rodent that lives in burrows. The squirrel eats seeds, fruits, and insects.

Hibernating in winter, the ground squirrel is seen in early spring. It is active in hot weather and does not seem to mind the excessive heat in the hottest months.

Fishhook Cactus

The small fishhook cactus grows in clumps. Its spines curve at the top like fishhooks. In spring, pink or lavender flowers ring its top.

I hope the music that I make
Will have "charms to soothe" this snake.
Otherwise, I think that he
Will try to "put the squeeze" on me.

Collared Peccary

The collared peccary, also called the javelina, is the only native pig-like animal in America. However, it is not a true pig.

The animal has black and gray bristles, sharp tusks, and a snout for rooting out insects and tubers.

It eats the fruits and pads of the prickly pear cactus, and also lizards and snakes.

Wolf

Rare in the Southwest in the United States because of continued persecution, the wolf is more common in Mexico.

This animal is heavily built, with a broad head and thick fur. It is about the size of a German shepherd dog.

The wolf prefers big game, but it will eat rodents, rabbits, and some carrion.

It lives in small family groups and is a devoted parent and a good provider.

These three pigs, the wolf will find,
Are not the fairy story kind.
When they're running in a pack,
He would be foolish to attack.

Gila Woodpecker

Common in the saguaro desert, the Gila woodpecker (sometimes called zebra-backed) is gray-brown in color, with a striped back and white wing patches. The male has a red patch on its head.

The woodpecker makes a hole in the saguaro cactus for its nest. This home is often taken over by other birds.

The woodpecker eats insects and cactus fruits.

Saguaro

Largest of all cacti in the United States, the saguaro may grow to over forty feet in height. It can weigh as much as ten tons. It often lives 150 years or more.

The saguaro has an accordion-like structure that allows the plant to swell during rainy periods, storing water, and to shrink during dry times.

Pima and Papago Indians gather the red pulpy fruit, which develops from the white flowers, and use it fresh or preserved. The fruit and seeds are also eaten by birds and other animals.

The saguaro blossom is the Arizona state flower.

Elf Owl

Smallest owl in the world, the elf owl is about the size of a sparrow. In the desert it nests in an abandoned woodpecker hole in a saguaro cactus. It is nocturnal and eats insects and scorpions.

The woodpecker is kind of irked,
Because for days he worked and worked
To make that hole just right in size —
Just for himself — not other guys!

Horned Lizard

Frequently called a horned toad, this animal is not a toad at all — but a lizard. A spiny flat-looking creature with a short tail, it is a wizard at camouflage and is hard to see on the desert floor.

The horned lizard is especially fond of ants.

When alarmed, the lizard can squirt blood from its eyes. It is a harmless creature, however, and is protected by law in Arizona.

Ant

In the Southwest are many species of ants. The ones you are most likely to notice are the harvester ants, because of the craters they build around the entrances to their underground dwellings. The harvester ants collect seeds for food.

There are thousands of kinds of ants in the world. The queens of the ant colonies are responsible for laying the eggs. Worker ants feed the queens and the colony, take care of the young, and defend the home.

It is not easy to ignore
The horned "toad" waiting at my door,
Especially when I know that he
Would like to make a meal of me.

Verdin

Not much larger than a hummingbird, this little fellow, the verdin, is often seen in thorny desert growth where he finds insects and caterpillars. He has a gray body, greenish-yellow head, and russet shoulders. His voice seems loud for his size.

His nest is large and oval-shaped and has an entrance on one side.

Raven

Two types of raven are found in the Southwest — the common raven and the white-necked raven. The common raven is a large black bird about two feet long. The white-necked raven is smaller and nearer the size of a common crow; he often is mistaken for the latter, especially in flight.

The hoarse croaks of the ravens may be heard as they soar in open country. These omnivorous birds also eat carrion. Their large loose nest is built of sticks.

Mistletoe

A parasitic plant, the mistletoe found in the cottonwood trees has gray-green leaves and white berries. It is commonly used as a Christmas decoration. Another type, which attacks trees of the pea family (ironwood, mesquite, and so forth) has pink berries that serve as a main food source for some desert birds.

Yes, I am tiny, I admit;
But I can go where you can't fit.
So rude ravens — off with you —
I have my little work to do.

Porcupine

A rodent, about thirty inches long, the porcupine is brownish in color, with white or yellowish guard hairs. He is equipped with thousands of quills. He is clumsy and slow and has poor eyesight, but he can defend himself adequately with his barbed quills and flailing tail, causing pain and injury to predators.

The porcupine can climb trees, and he likes tender inner bark when it is available. He also eats low-growing shrubs, grasses, and mesquite beans.

Barrel Cactus

Because the barrel cactus grows faster on its shaded side, it usually leans to the southwest, and is therefore sometimes called a compass cactus.

The barrel cactus does not contain clear water, as some believe. However, by cutting open the barrel and mashing the pulp to a slimy liquid, one may obtain moisture — if in dire need.

The flowers of the barrel cactus range from yellow to pink. The fruits are eaten by birds and other animals.

Prairie Dog

Like the coyote, the prairie dog is a symbol of the Old West. Prairie dogs once were abundant, but due to severe exterminating programs, they have become a rarity.

Prairie dogs dig underground cities, with tunnels extending long distances. This helps conserve rainwater.

Their food is mainly plants and also some insects.

The porcupine appears nearsighted.
His love, I fear, is unrequited.
The cactus spines have him confused,
And his friends seem quite amused.

Field Cricket

Field crickets are black or brown and about an inch long. They are nocturnal and noisiest when the weather is hot. They scrape their wings together to make their sound. They don't really listen in "de" feet, they listen in "de" leg. Their hearing organs are in their front legs.

Crickets are primarily plant eaters.

Couch's Spadefoot Toad

After summer rains have fallen, and ponds have been formed, the spadefoot toads appear in great numbers. Eggs are laid in ponds and develop rapidly. Toads' mating calls fill the night with a sad *baa*-ing sound.

Spadefoots survive drought by burrowing deep into the ground. They are equipped with horny structures on the soles of their feet to aid in digging. When they burrow, they move backward into the ground; they may stay in their burrows many weeks or months.

These toads are active mostly at night.

The crickets' chirping is in vain,
When Mr. Toad croaks his refrain.
With his noise, they can't compete,
So they listen in defeat.

Burrowing Owl

Whereas most owls are busy at night, this small, long-legged bird is active in daylight hours.

This owl eats insects and scorpions, a few lizards and small mammals, but principally grasshoppers.

The burrowing owl uses abandoned rodent burrows in the ground for his nest, frequently in a location where grasshoppers are abundant.

Cactus Wren

The state bird of Arizona, the cactus wren is the largest wren in the Southwest. It is brown, with spots of white and black, and with noticeable white eye stripes.

The nests of these birds are seen in many cholla cactus plants, because, it is believed, these spiny plants give good protection from enemies. For further precaution, wrens build decoy nests, which may lure predators away from the nest that holds the eggs.

These industrious birds are seen constantly on the run, looking for insects and poking and prying into every nook and crevice.

The cactus wren likes cholla best
To get protection for her nest.
"No stickery nests for me," says owl.
"I am a burrow-living fowl."

CHUCK
WAGGIN

Curved-billed Thrasher

An aggressive bird, gray-brown with fierce-looking red-orange eyes, the curve-billed thrasher will take over feeding places where other birds are eating. His voice sounds like a human whistle for attention, but he also has a pleasant song. The thrasher's bulky nest is made of twigs in cactus or mesquite.

Banded Sand Snake (top left)

A pale-yellow to red reptile, with dark bands usually encircling his body, the banded sand snake is about ten inches long. This harmless sand-burrowing snake emerges mostly at night. Its food consists of insects and probably ant pupae.

Sonoran Coral Snake (coming over upper rock)

The Sonoran coral snake is about eighteen inches long. It has brilliant bands of red, yellow, and black completely encircling the body, the red bands bordered on each side by the yellow ones. Related to the cobra, this snake has poisonous venom. However, the coral snake is shy and docile, spending much of its time below ground. Primarily nocturnal, the coral snake hunts for lizards and small snakes.

Sonoran Shovel-nosed Snake (coming over lower rock)

Because the colors of the Sonoran shovel-nosed snake are arranged in the same sequence as those of the Sonoran coral snake, one is often mistaken for the other. However, the shovel-nosed snake is harmless. On this snake the red bands do not encircle the body, and the back of the head is black. A similar species is the Western shovel-nosed snake. The shovel-nosed snake is nocturnal. Its food includes insects, spiders, scorpions, and centipedes.

Mountain King Snake (lower)

The mountain king snake is red, black, and white banded, with the red bands bordered by the black. The snout is whitish or flecked with white. It is a mountain dweller from chaparral zones to pine forests. This snake, a constrictor, takes lizards, snakes, and rodents as food. It is harmless to humans.

Their bands are black and red and yellow;
Among them is a harmful fellow.
Which one is the venomous snake?
Be careful now; make no mistake.

Vinegaroon (right)

The vinegaroon, or whip-tailed scorpion, is a harmless creature with a long whip-like tail. When disturbed or injured it can eject a substance that smells like vinegar. It eats cockroaches and other insects, and spiders.

Ocotillo

A plant with long slender thorny stems, the ocotillo grows eight to twelve feet high. In the spring, bright red blossoms appear at the tips of the stems. After rains, small leaves are put forth. When the soil is dry, the leaves fall off. This plant may grow several sets of leaves each year — a new set after each rain. It is not a cactus.

Buffalo Gourd

A plant that grows along desert washes, the buffalo gourd is relished by many desert creatures. This plant has yellow trumpet-shaped blossoms and globular striped fruits.

Desert Gray Fox

The desert gray fox is a small animal with a black-tipped bushy tail and a gray coat with orange, black, and white markings. Usually this fox hunts at night, looking for rodents, small mammals, fruits, and berries. He can climb trees.

Scorpion (left)

Largest scorpion in the Southwest, the giant hairy scorpion gives a painful but seldom dangerous sting. The small rock scorpion, straw-colored and slender, is considered dangerous to humans but — under ordinary circumstances — only to children under six years and adults in poor health. Scorpions eat moths, spiders, caterpillars, and many kinds of insects.

The desert fox looks so alert,
At those strange creatures in the dirt.
He wonders which one has the sting
And which one is the harmless thing.

Red-tailed Hawk

The red-tailed hawk is a soaring bird with a wing spread of about four feet. Its tail is reddish above and whitish pink beneath. Often seen perched on a pole, the hawk swoops from high in the air to snatch up its prey — rabbits and mice, and occasionally small birds and snakes. Its nest is a platform of sticks in an isolated tree or saguaro.

Joshua Tree

Largest of the yuccas, the Joshua tree may grow to thirty feet or more. It is a member of the lily family, and produces greenish white flowers from February to April.

Joshua Tree National Monument is in California, but the trees also grow in the northwestern and west-central parts of Arizona.

Scott's Oriole

Scott's oriole is a yellow bird with a black head, back, and throat, and a tail that is black with yellow sides. The female is more of a greenish-yellow. The oriole has a pleasing song, suggestive of the meadow lark's song.

This bird makes a grassy pouchlike nest in a Joshua tree. It eats caterpillars, insects, and fruits.

Another oriole found in the Southwest is the hooded oriole, a bird that prefers palm trees for nesting.

Hare

In the United States the hare generally is called a rabbit. However, the jackrabbit is really a hare. It is a large, swift, timid animal, and is prey for many carnivores.

A red-tailed hawk, up in the air,
Spots the fleeing, frightened hare.
It may be safe 'neath Joshua trees;
So, in haste, hare heads for these.

[70]

Pronghorn Antelope

The pronghorn antelope has a tan coat with white underparts and white rump patch. The antelope can signal danger by erecting the white rump hairs that can be seen for great distances by others of his herd. This animal can run more than fifty miles an hour. It has keen eyesight. Its food is vegetation.

Jackrabbit

Two species of jackrabbit found in Arizona are the black-tailed jackrabbit and the antelope jackrabbit, the latter so called because it flashes a white rump patch like that of the pronghorn antelope. These hares are noted for speed. Their long powerful legs aid in long leaps away from a pursuer. Jackrabbits are vegetarians.

Zebra-tailed Lizard

A gray lizard with a flat tail and long slender legs, the zebra-tailed lizard is adapted for running at great speed. He and the collared lizards are probably the speediest of all lizards. The tail, often held curled over the back, has black bars on its white underside. This lizard, like some others, can grow another tail if he loses his to a predator.

"Slow down and live," we humans advise.
But for these creatures, that slogan's unwise.
Their greatest defense is their great speed —
In case of attack, a blessing indeed.

Gilded Flicker

The gilded flicker is a woodpecker about ten inches long, with a brown back, spotted breast with a black bib, and a golden color under the wings. The male has a red mustache. The bill is strong and pointed, for drilling into trees and cacti.

The flicker's nest is in a hole in a saguaro or cottonwood tree. Its food consists of insects and wild fruits and seeds.

Beaver

The Southwest's largest rodent, the yellow-brown beaver, weighs thirty to fifty pounds. He has a naked, scaly, paddle-shaped tail, which he uses to slap the water loudly to warn of enemies.

The beaver works mostly at night. He eats water plants and the bark off the trees that he gnaws down to build his dams. The beaver lodge is built in the dam far enough from shore that he can escape to it from enemies by diving into the water.

Petrified Wood

Huge trees have been turned from living things into stone over a period of millions of years. They have been fossilized with mineral-bearing water (mostly silica) that seeped into the wood tissue while the trees were buried in mud and sand.

Erosion has uncovered the long-buried trees, and we see some of them again exposed, but in stone form and brilliantly colored by minerals.

Flicker says, "I bent my bill
When a hole I tried to drill.
So beaver, do not gnaw this wood;
It will do your teeth no good."

Turkey Vulture

A black bird with a small naked red head and a wingspread of six feet, the turkey vulture soars in wide arcs in the sky. With its phenomenal eyesight, it can spot food from great heights. A carrion eater, this bird is valuable as a scavenger; for that reason it is protected. This bird is usually silent, but it hisses when cornered.

Velvet Ant

The velvet ant, with its red to yellow-white dense hair, resembles a bit of colored fuzz. This insect is a female wingless wasp, which packs a painful sting. She lays her eggs in nests of other wasps or bees, and her young become parasites on the original occupant's larvae.

Desert Cottontail

The desert cottontail is gray-white with patches of yellow-brown. Each day of his life is in peril, as almost every carnivore preys on him. If he is being pursued, he has no defense except to dash in a zigzag course to the nearest brush pile or clump of thorns where the predators cannot follow. The cottontail makes its nest in a shallow depression scratched out in the ground and lined with grass and tufts of fur.

Dust Devil

A sure sign of summer is the miniature whirlwind that skips through the desert.

The vulture is a homely creature,
But he is a desert feature.
He should never be demeaned,
For he keeps the desert cleaned.

Jaguar

Largest and most powerful member of the American cat family, the jaguar is deep yellow to tawny with black rosettes. He has a long heavy tail and short muscular legs.

This is one cat that enjoys water and does not hesitate to cross streams or take baths. He eats peccaries, deer, and birds, and he also likes fish.

Tumbleweed

The tumbleweed is a native of Asia. The most common species is the Russian thistle. The weed is green in summer when other desert weeds are brown. When it dries it is blown about by the winds, and in this way its seeds are scattered.

Badger

The badger has a long coat of grizzled gray hair and black and white markings on his head. He has a heavy body and short legs, with long claws that make him a champion digger. When molested he can dig himself out of sight in no time. When he can't hide, he is fearless and a fierce powerful fighter.

This animal lives in a burrow. His food consists of rodents, eggs, reptiles, insects, and birds. He may be seen in daylight hours, but is most active at night.

The jaguar wonders why the speed.
That round thing's just a tumbleweed.
In truth, the badger's very brave,
But he'd as soon be in his cave.

Grasshopper Mouse

The grasshopper mouse, sometimes called a scorpion mouse, is five to seven inches long, with a heavy body, a short thick tapered tail, and short legs.

Like bloodhounds, these mice stalk their prey by scent. These carnivorous creatures prey on other mice — even their own kind. They prefer grasshoppers for food, but also like scorpions.

Barn Owl

Because of his facial outline, the barn owl is sometimes called a monkey-faced owl. Of all the owls in Arizona this one is the lightest in color. It has small dark eyes and long legs. Unlike some owls, it "doesn't give a hoot," but more of a screech or hiss. The barn owl is a valuable bird because it helps keep the rodent population in check.

Teddy Bear Cholla

When the sun shines on the teddy bear cholla, it looks soft and luminous. This silvery green cactus has pale yellow-green flowers. The cactus joints will dislodge at the slightest touch, and the barbs are painful and difficult to remove from flesh. In other words, "these teddy bears aren't for huggin'."

Where the joints fall, they take root, forming new plants.

These little mice have been pursued,
But they have managed to elude
This owl, whose hungry eyes are glued
On them — his very favorite food.

Kit Fox

Smallest of the North American foxes, the kit fox weighs four to six pounds. Also called the desert swift, because of its swift speed, this yellow-gray animal has large sensitive ears and a bushy tail tipped in black.

This little fox lives in a burrow that has several exits for escape. Its home is usually in a sandy location. The kangaroo rat and other rodents — the kit fox's chief food — also make their homes in these sandy places.

Hog-nosed Skunk

The hog-nosed skunk has coarse short hair that is white from the top of the head, along the back, and over the entire tail, with the rest of the hair black.

This animal has a long flexible snout that enables it to get at insects underground. The heavy claws on the front feet also aid in this endeavor. The food that the skunk likes best consists of insects, worms, and larvae; but it will also eat fruits, eggs, and rodents. The skunk is usually nocturnal.

The hog-nosed skunk uses his snout
To root insects and larvae out.
I'm not surprised — no not one whit —
That now and then his nose gets bit!

Great Horned Owl

The great horned owl, sometimes called a cat owl, is the desert's largest owl. It has a wing span of over four feet, is nearly two feet long, and has feathered ear tufts, big round yellow eyes, and powerful talons and beak.

This owl makes its nest in a cliff or canyon, sometimes taking an old nest of a hawk or a crow for its own. Flying on silent wings, the owl catches many rabbits and mice.

Mountain Sheep

Mountain sheep have hair like deer instead of wool like domestic sheep. The rams, weighing 200 pounds or more, are gray-brown with white rump patches, and have massive curled horns.

These sheep live in desert mountain areas inaccessible to most other animals. The concave cloven hoofs of the mountain sheep make for sure footing on rocky terrain, where it is difficult for predators to follow.

These sheep browse on desert shrubs and cactus fruits, eating grass when it is available.

Palo Verde

The trunk, branches, and limbs of the palo verde tree are all green. A golden cloud of yellow blossoms appears in the spring. The two common species of this tree are the blue palo verde with blue-green bark and bright yellow flowers, and the foothill palo verde with pale yellow flowers.

The words *palo verde* in Spanish mean *green stick*.

The palo verde tree is the Arizona state tree.

"Hoo's that crossing overhead
And ruining my sleep?"
"Don't you fret," the lambkin said,
"We're just some mountain sheep."

Hummingbird

The males of most species of hummingbird have jewel-like throat feathers. These hummers have long slim bills and long tongues for sipping nectar and for snatching insects.

Hummingbirds can fly backward, or go straight up in the air, or hover.

These tiny creatures build neat nests, about the size of a half walnut shell, constructed of plant down and cobwebs. The eggs are about the size of navy beans.

Many species of hummingbird visit the Southwest; some come in winter, some come in summer, and others are merely transients.

Fringe-toed Sand Lizard

Sand lizards, who live in dunes, are light tan with black markings. The fringes of the lizard's toes make it possible for him to "swim" in the sand. These lizards can bury themselves in the sand, disappearing in the wink of an eye. Nasal valves are a help in breathing under sand. These lizards are chiefly insectivorous.

Desert Tobacco

Tree tobacco grows ten to twelve feet in height and has large leaves and tubular yellow flowers. Hummingbirds are attracted to the trumpetlike flowers.

A smaller type of desert tobacco plant grows from one to three feet in height. It has greenish white flowers. The Indians have smoked this tobacco at some of their rituals.

Bright as any jewel or gem,
We never tire of watching them.
Iridescent feathers bright,
Gleam and glow in the sunlight.

Tarantula Hawk

The tarantula hawk, or pepsis wasp, is a large wasp with a blue-black body and bright red-orange wings. This wasp is sometimes seen scurrying over the desert in search of a tarantula.

The wasp stings and paralyzes the spider, but she does not kill it. She then drags the victim to a burrow, where she lays an egg on it. After the egg is hatched, the still living spider will serve as fresh food for the larva.

Rock Squirrel

The rock squirrel resembles a tree squirrel. It is about eighteen inches long and has a long bushy tail. Its general color is gray, with mottled back and sides.

The rock squirrel lives in a burrow in a rocky area in the foothills or on a mountain slope. Its food is insects, seeds, nuts and fruits, and occasionally a bird or small rodent.

Christmas Cholla

A slender-jointed bushy cactus, the Christmas cholla, or tesajo, grows to two feet or more. The small yellow-green blossoms in May or June are not very noticeable. However, the red-orange fruit, about an inch long and very conspicuous, appears in the fall and winter months. The cactus is therefore aptly called a Christmas cholla.

[88]

In zigzag course that was ever wider,
The wasp came running, while squirrel eyed her.
She peered into holes that might provide her
A tarantula, our largest spider.

Desert Lily

The desert lily, or ajo, resembles the Easter lily. The plant has fragrant white flowers that bloom from February to May.

The bulbs of the desert lily have a smell and taste resembling that of garlic. The name *ajo* means garlic in Spanish. The town of Ajo in southern Arizona was named for this plant. The bulbs of the plant grow deep in the ground, eighteen inches or more in sandy soil.

Hooded Skunk

The hooded skunk is found in varying color patterns of black and white — from nearly all black with white side stripes, to black with all white back and tail. The hair on the neck usually spreads out into a ruff.

This skunk feeds on insects, vegetation, reptiles, and small mammals. Its den is usually in a rock crevice. The animal is primarily nocturnal, but it may be seen in the daytime.

The hooded skunk is found in southwestern New Mexico, southern Arizona, and south through Mexico.

Pocket Gopher

A generally dark brown or reddish brown rodent, the pocket gopher grows from seven to twelve inches in length. He has a heavy body, a short tail, and forefeet equipped with long sharp claws for digging burrows. He spends most of his time underground, where he feeds on bulbs, roots, and stems of plants.

Eighteen inches down below
Grows the bulb of this ajo.
And I am sure that you can tell
It has a garlic taste and smell.

Screech Owl

A small, predominantly gray bird with feathered ear tufts, the screech owl nests in a saguaro hole or a tree cavity. Its food is mostly insects, scorpions, and millipedes, with some rodents. This owl does not screech; its song is a quavering whistle.

Nighthawk

The nighthawk is a relative of the whippoorwill. It has a small bill, but with its huge mouth it scoops up nocturnal insects on the fly, soaring and diving almost to the ground, and veering upward again as it chases its prey. It can sometimes be seen catching insects around bright city lights.

Long-tongued Bat

A medium-sized bat, the long-tongued bat has a face resembling that of a fox. It has an erect nose leaf and a long tongue, enabling it to feast in cactus flowers. In this way the bat helps pollinate the saguaro cactus. By day it roosts in caves and rock crevices.

Desert Sunset

Each desert day is likely to end with a spectacular sunset that is a photographer's or an artist's dream. Every evening a new show is to be seen — each one a sight never to be forgotten.

The sun goes down, and nightfall brings
All manner of night-flying things —
The screech owl and the nectar bats,
Nighthawks showing off like acrobats.

Coyote

A doglike animal with light brown fur sprinkled with gray or black, the coyote is important in nature's scheme of things. He preys on weak or diseased creatures; he is a scavenger and carrion eater; and he is an important check on rabbits and rodents.

The coyote is cunning, sly, and intelligent. He is a prevalent and thriving animal in the Southwest, despite man's attempts to eliminate him. He makes his home in a burrow or a cave.

The howl of the coyote is a symbol of the Old West. The animal is especially vocal on moonlight nights.

Night-blooming Cereus (right)

The night-blooming cereus has a stem that looks like a nondescript, sprawling, dead-looking stick often going unnoticed until the flowers appear. The root is a large water-storing tuber. The plant grows inconspicuously beneath bushes.

In June or July the plant suddenly produces beautiful white blossoms that open almost before your very eyes. These blooms have a fragrant perfume that fills the desert night with its aroma. The blooms last just one night.

"Gee, we wish you'd stop that yapping!
Don't you know that we are napping?"
His howl is famous in the West,
But prairie dogs think he's a pest.